Original title:
In the Shade of the Orchard

Copyright © 2025 Creative Arts Management OÜ
All rights reserved.

Author: Amelia Montgomery
ISBN HARDBACK: 978-1-80586-378-6
ISBN PAPERBACK: 978-1-80586-850-7

The Cool Embrace of Green

Beneath the leafy boughs we play,
The squirrels hold a nutty ballet.
With every crunch, our laughter grows,
While hidden critters strike a pose.

The sun peeks through, doing a jig,
A hare hops by, wearing a twig.
Oh, what a ruckus, what a sight,
Nature's jesters, pure delight!

Fruitful Reveries

The apples giggle, round and red,
Telling tales of what they said.
Pears are gossiping, sweet and ripe,
While grapes form clusters, oh so hype.

Bananas slip in with a grin,
Challenging each other to spin.
In this patch of whimsy and cheer,
Every fruit has a joke to hear!

Shadows Dance with Light

The sun sways low, casting a joke,
As shadows stretch and softly poke.
The grass blades giggle, tickled by air,
While lazy bees buzz without a care.

A rooster struts, a feathery jest,
Claiming mornings as he knows best.
In this garden, laughter takes flight,
Under an umbrella of warmth and light!

A Serenade of Sprouts

Tiny sprouts sing in the breeze,
In harmony with rustling leaves.
They twist and curl, vying for cheer,
Each with a story for all to hear.

Carrots boast of their roots so deep,
While radishes wink, secrets to keep.
This veggie chorus, oh what fun,
In every row, laughter is spun!

The Orchard's Hidden Heart

Beneath the boughs, the squirrels play,
With acorns tossed in merry fray.
They chatter loud, they leap and dive,
While pondering how to best survive.

A grumpy owl gives a sleepy leer,
As raccoons dance, fueled by cheer.
A game of tag on branches sways,
Nature's jesters in the sun's soft rays.

Beneath Blossoms and Breezes

Pigs in shades of pink, they prance,
Beneath a tree, they find romance.
They snuffle and snort, a curious crew,
While bees buzz loudly, 'What's all this goo?'

The breeze brings laughter, tickles noses,
As flowers giggle, striking poses.
With petals twirling, worms in glee,
Who knew that gardening could be so free?

The Language of Leaves

A leaf whispers secrets in rustling tones,
Sharing tales of squirrels and their silly loans.
They barter nuts like seasoned pros,
In contracts written with twiggy prose.

Gnarled hands of branches clap in delight,
As shadows dance, a comical sight.
The sun plays peekaboo, and oh, what fun!
In this leafy world, we're never done.

Nectar of Nostalgia

A fruit flies past, a humorous buzz,
It hits a frog, who says, 'What was that? Buzz!'
They laugh and joke about the time,
When ants staged plays, oh what a crime!

Jars of jam sit upon the shelf,
Reminding us of our silly selves.
With sticky fingers, we share the taste,
Of sweet memories, never a waste.

In the Arms of the Apple Trees

Beneath the boughs, I spun around,
My shoe got stuck, I hit the ground.
The apples snicker, what a sight!
They whispered secrets, day turned night.

I climbed up high, thought I'd be cool,
But learned too late, it's just a fool.
The branches waved, they played a game,
While I yelled out, 'Who's to blame?'

Where Time Seems to Stand Still

A clock forgot to tick away,
As crickets laughed and joined the play.
The sun wore goggles, oh so bright,
While squirrels danced with sheer delight.

I tried to nap beneath a pear,
But bees had plans, they buzzed with flair.
They tossed my hat, they took my snack,
And I came home with quite the quack.

Chasing the Fragrance of Spring

The flowers opened wide their grin,
While bees performed a buzzing spin.
I chased a scent, so sweet, divine,
But tripped on roots and fell in line.

The cats nearby took up the chase,
As petals danced, they joined the race.
The gardener laughed, his hat awry,
'Next time, kid, just walk nearby!'

Conversations with the Wind

The breeze came in, it blew my hat,
It whispered tales of this and that.
I tried to speak, but left a burp,
The wind just chuckled, gave a chirp.

It carried off my plans for lunch,
And swirled away with quite the punch.
I shouted back, but it was gone,
The trees just giggled at my con.

Sun-kissed Whispers

Beneath the boughs, where laughter grows,
Squirrels argue, nobody knows.
Apples giggle, peaches tease,
A tomato's blush in the warm breeze.

Bumblebees buzz a silly tune,
While shadows dance beneath the moon.
A melon rolled, it took a tumble,
With every thud, the orchard rumbled.

Sunflowers wave in the light so bright,
Trying to win in a fashion fight.
They whisper secrets to the pears,
About silly hats and funky stares.

Fruit flies gather, plan their spree,
Throw a picnic on a cherry tree.
They laugh and snack on juicy treats,
In this giggling world, they take their seats.

Serene Retreat Among the Branches

Underneath the leafy dome,
Birds debate which is their home.
Crickets chirp, they sing out loud,
While a rabbit shows off, oh so proud.

Peaches drop in a plump parade,
Rolling down like a small charade.
They compete for the best red hat,
While ducks waddle past, tipping their mat.

A wise old owl hoots a joke,
It's so bad, the vines almost choke.
Ripe figs giggle, swaying with glee,
As they dance beneath the old apple tree.

This merry haven is quite a sight,
Where fruits and critters share delight.
But be aware if laughter's loud,
A plum might join in, feeling proud!

The Painter's Palette of Nature

Brushstrokes made by sunlit beams,
Colors burst in joyful dreams.
A canvas rich with vie and cheer,
As oranges clown with a sneaky pear.

Grapes wear coats of purple shine,
While lemons throw pies, oh so fine.
Citrus laughter fills the air,
Making even radishes declare!

Blushing berries play hide and seek,
With butterflies, both sly and sleek.
A rainbow feast on every line,
Nature's art, oh so divine!

As branches sway and laughter flies,
The orchard hums beneath blue skies.
And when the day begins to fade,
A fruit parade promises charades!

A Retreat of Fruits and Folklore

An apple told a tale so grand,
Of juicy treasures across the land.
"He said, she said," the berries chirped,
While a nut fell off, looking perturbed.

A carrot dreamed it was a star,
A fruit flew by, yelling, "How bizarre!"
Tomatoes rolled with giggles bright,
Claiming they'd win the veggie fight.

Beneath the trees, where shadows play,
Fruits share stories at the end of day.
Cucumbers argue who should lead,
As salad leaves plan a daring deed.

In this retreat of mischievous glee,
Folklore tales grow on every tree.
So come on down for a laugh or two,
You'll find a world that's full of woo!

Shadowed Retreats of Repose

Beneath the branches, squirrels play,
They chatter loud, they steal my clay.
With puzzled glances, I just stare,
Wondering why they're so debonair.

A picnic basket lies in wait,
But ants arrive to seal my fate.
They march like soldiers on a quest,
As I laugh at their tiny pest fest.

The fruit hangs low, a tempting sight,
But swings and ropes give quite a fright.
With giggles shared, our plans unfold,
As laughter spreads, a sight to behold.

So here I sit, in light and shade,
With fruit and friends, we've got it made.
The world can wait, let nature thrive,
In this retreat, we feel alive.

The Song of Falling Leaves

Leaves fall down like little stars,
They twirl and spin from tree-top bars.
A crafty breeze joins in the fun,
As I dodge the rain from the golden sun.

With a rustle here and a crinkle there,
A dance-off starts, without a care.
I twirl and trip on leaves so bright,
And laugh out loud at my silly plight.

The ground's a quilt of colors bold,
Where stories of autumn dreams are told.
With every step, a crumple blooms,
While nature sings in playful tunes.

So join the dance, don't be shy,
For these fallen friends know how to fly.
A frolic through gold, with each hearty laugh,
In this leafy world, we share the path.

A Kingdom of Roots and Fruit

In roots below, a kingdom thrives,
With wiggly worms and busy hives.
A pumpkin king, with ghostly grin,
Lurks in shadows where tales begin.

The grapefruits giggle on the vine,
Sharing secrets of rot and wine.
The apples roll with cider dreams,
While peaches blush, bursting at seams.

A crow delivers laughs each day,
With caws that make the orchard sway.
Jokes on chickens flying high,
With berry pies that wink and sigh.

In this land, where mischief rules,
Nature's jesters, wise like fools.
With laughter ripe, we join the spree,
In harmony, a jester's jubilee.

Dappled Glimpses of Paradise

Amid the dappled light we roam,
With giggles bouncing like a foam.
A fairy tale beneath the tree,
Where shadows dance and spirits flee.

The bees hum tunes of honey gold,
While hidden jokes start to unfold.
I stretch to reach that juicy prize,
As laughter spills from silly sighs.

A rogue banana slips my shoe,
And with a splat, I'm greased anew.
While chorus sprouts from all around,
With every fall, a joy is found.

Yet in this space, we find our glee,
As nature sings our symphony.
With friendships shared, and snacks in hand,
In sunny joys, we make our stand.

Under the Weight of Fruit-laden Dreams

Apples tumble from the trees,
Squirrels dance with utmost ease.
They think they're kings, a brave brigade,
While I just stand in fruit parade.

Peaches weigh my branches down,
They're fruiting kings, I wear a crown.
But when I walk, oh what a sight,
I trip and land, oh what a fright!

Grapes giggle as they swing so low,
Chasing sunbeams, they steal the show.
"Look at me!" the berries shout,
While I dodge splashes from their clout.

The fruit brigade, a jolly crew,
Make merry mischief, it's all true.
They laugh and roll from tree to ground,
In this harvest, joy is found.

Sanctuary of the Sweetened Breeze

Lemonade dreams in every breeze,
Where citrus creaks and giggles tease.
I'm caught in laughter, ripe with zest,
As squirrels host a fruity fest.

Bananas swing, and cherries cheer,
The fruit parade grows ever near.
I'd join the revelry, but wait!
My hat just flew; it's quite the fate!

Watermelons slide with flair,
While grasshoppers leap without a care.
Each juicy burst, a silly joke,
As I trip over, oh, the poke!

A kite of mangoes drifts up high,
Trying to take off, oh my, oh my!
They soar like dreams, or maybe flies,
In this sweet place beneath the skies.

Beneath the Boughs of Abundance

Peaches plop, and laughter roams,
I find my feet, make peace with gnome.
"Step right up!" the cherries sing,
As I fall down amidst the spring.

Oranges mock with every squeeze,
As bees buzz by with sticky knees.
I try to dance, they all do laugh,
Guess I'm the punchline of the staff!

Under the apples, secrets keep,
While turtles snooze and critters leap.
But why's the pumpkin rolling here?
It seems today, it's all quite clear!

Banana peels are out to play,
And tumbleweeds will lead the way.
With giggles echoing all around,
I'm just a fool on fruit ground.

Whispers of Ripening Fruit

The cherries whisper, "Can you hear?"
They giggle softly, stay quite near.
"Tell us secrets, share your woes,"
I grin and nod as the laughter flows.

A watermelon laughs, "Crack me wide!"
As friends recount what fruit can hide.
But one big shove, whoops! Down I fall,
The orchard's laughter echoes call.

Pears gossip sweet with every breeze,
"Look, our friend's stuck like a tease!"
Tomatoes snicker from the vine,
As I'm wrapped up in ivy twine!

But joy doth flourish in this place,
Where every fruit brings a smiling face.
In this moment, full of cheer,
I'm the fool, but who's to sneer?

A Tapestry of Leaves

Leaves whisper secrets, quite absurd,
As squirrels debate who's the best bird.
A butterfly stumbles, lands on a toe,
And giggles erupt; oh, what a show.

Sunlight flickers, a tickling sprout,
While rabbits play tag, they jump about.
The apple tree grumbles, 'I'm not a pie!'
But who can resist that juicy supply?

Breezes carry laughter, so silly and sweet,
As the ants throw a dance with two left feet.
The gardener chuckles, potting his joy,
In every odd corner, there's giggles to enjoy.

The Gentle Caress of Nature

A caterpillar slides, what's his big dream?
To one day be bold and to fly, it would seem.
But every time he tries, he falls headlong,
Nature just laughs; it's all part of the song.

The sun pokes fun, 'You're crawling too slow!'
While the ladybugs dance in a fancy slow show.
A breeze woos the flowers, they blush and swirl,
And bees miss their mark—oh, the buzz they unfurl!

In this green playhouse, where mischief is rife,
Even the pears giggle at ordinary life.
If laughter's the fruit, then it's ripe on the vine,
Join nature's parade, it's simply divine!

Fruits of Yesterday's Memories

Ripe figs once tossed, a forgotten old game,
Now the garden gnomes have joined in the fame.
With plums in their hats, they bob and they sway,
While recalling the jest of their youthful day.

Cherries chime in with a jingle so bright,
Painted red faces in afternoon light.
A berry brigade leads the parade with flair,
Playing hopscotch while hanging mid-air!

From past fruity follies, they gather around,
Telling tall tales of the mischief they found.
Embracing the laughter, they slide down the lane,
The orchard remembers, but never feels pain.

Twilight Among the Trees

As twilight draws in, the chatter is grand,
Crickets compose for the last summer band.
A squirrel in a tux, what a dapper sight,
He thinks he can dance, but it ends in a flight.

Fireflies flicker like stars, oh what fun,
Trading secrets with shadows, nowhere to run.
A beehive's gossip, it stings with delight,
As they plan the next picnic down by moonlight.

Old oaks make snickers at a raccoon's plight,
Trying to steal berries, but oh what a fright!
With laughter echoing 'neath the canopy high,
Nature's own comedy, under the sky.

Beneath the Arching Branches

Squirrels plotting with acorn crowns,
While birds gossip in rhythm and sounds.
A rogue apple falls with a thud,
Laughing at gravity's messy flood.

Breezes dance with mischievous flair,
Grass tickles toes, a delightful affair.
Children giggle, dodging the bees,
Chasing dreams on a warm, sunny breeze.

The Promise of Forgotten Seasons

A pumpkin tries to squeeze in a pear,
"Just one more!" it cries, but no one's aware.
The cherry tree sighs, full of sweet pride,
While the peach rolls away like it's trying to hide.

Yesterday's blooms still cling to the space,
Whispering secrets with shimmery grace.
Nutty debates about who's the best,
As apples just sit, musing on rest.

A Constellation of Leaves

Leaves gossip softly about their own hue,
"I'm more brilliant!" the maple coos too.
While the elm tries to outgrow the sass,
"Hold my branch, watch my bravado surpass!"

Under the stars where shadows do tease,
Nature's own laughter floats with the breeze.
A tale of twigs and ridiculous tricks,
Even the roots get caught in the mix.

The Orchard's Quiet Respite

In this calm refuge, a raccoon with flair,
Wears his collection of hats without care.
A fox critiques with a stylish nod,
"Your fashion choices are simply quite odd!"

The sun stretches out, a lazy old cat,
While the grass grins at the sight of that.
A picnic awaits, yet ants have a plan,
To steal our lunch—oh, but they can't!

Cradle of Aliveness

Beneath the boughs, the squirrels tease,
They mock the bees and dance with ease.
A rabbit hops, it trips and giggles,
While ants parade in tiny wiggles.

The sun beams down, a golden crown,
As children laugh and tumble down.
A dog rolls 'round, he finds a stick,
And with a bark, this makes him tick.

A picnic spread, what a delight,
But ants join in, they take a bite!
A sandwich flies, a fruit takes flight,
It's chaos amidst pure delight!

The warmth invites all creatures near,
Even a frog who jumps with cheer.
In this wild, and silly play,
Life's painted bright in every sway.

Secrets Woven in Petal and Leaf

Whispers float on the gentle breeze,
As flowers gossip 'bout the bees.
A daisy winks at a shy rose,
'What secrets do your petals pose?'

The ivy climbs with a sly intent,
While mushrooms chuckle, so well-bent.
A butterfly flutters, all aglow,
'Did you hear? The daisies put on a show!'

Under the canopies, laughter rings,
As the breeze plays tunes of silly things.
The trees chat softly, branch to branch,
'Let's plan a leaf-waltz, shall we dance?'

A juicy rumor they spin around,
Of hidden treasures beneath the ground.
Each petal, each leaf, all in good jest,
Life in the garden, a comic quest!

A Walk Among Golden Hues

Golden sunflowers stand so bright,
They bow and sway, what a funny sight!
A bumblebee buzzes with flair,
While a butterfly lands with gentle care.

Here come the kids, with frisbees galore,
Chasing the wind, they tumble and soar.
A dog, in glee, is chasing his tail,
While a cat observes, plotting to fail.

Each fruit tree stirs, with laughter loud,
As plump apples sway, feeling proud.
A pear drops down and rolls away,
All the while, the lemons betray!

The berries share, in lipstick pink,
Their juicy tales—they laugh and wink.
Oh what joy in golden hues,
A day filled not with old but new!

Meditations in the Orchard

Sitting beneath a tree of glee,
A wise old owl hoots, 'Come sit with me!'
The apples giggle, they dance on high,
As a breeze whispers, 'Give me a try!'

A squirrel reads a book on a limb,
Its pages flutter, it's hard to skim.
Rabbits debate the best salad dress,
While a fox shares tales of his own finesse.

Each leaf shares wisdom in rustling song,
Reminding us here, we all belong.
Laughter echoes, a melodic cheer,
In the orchard's heart, there's nothing to fear!

With fruits all around, I munch and smile,
Life's simple joys stretch on for miles.
These meditations, so sweet and bright,
Turn every day into pure delight.

Lullabies in the Orchard

The apples giggle in the breeze,
While pears joke, "What's up with the trees?"
Cherries blush when neighbors laugh,
Plums roll on ground for a silly bath.

A worm recites a cheesy rhyme,
As he scoots through the leaves, so sublime.
"I'm the king of this fruity land,"
But falls flat—his reign was unplanned.

The sun tickles each leaf's cheek,
While oranges play hide and seek.
The laughter spreads from tree to tree,
As the fruit brigade dances with glee!

Dreams of jam swirl all about,
In this kooky place, there's no doubt.
With each chuckle, the juice runs sweet,
In our funny grove, life's a treat!

Fruits, Shadows, and Serenity

Bananas swing from branches high,
Saying, "Why not reach for the sky?"
Lemons crack jokes; they're so tart,
While figs play the quiet one's part.

In the twilight, shadows prance,
With every flicker, we take a chance.
"Did you hear about the grape so bold?"
He wore a sweater made of gold!

A cantaloupe takes a quirky seat,
Chilling out with a funky beat.
"Let's throw a party, this is grand,"
And soon we're dancing, hand in hand.

Beneath the laughs, we find some peace,
In this orchard where joy won't cease.
As twilight wraps around us tight,
We'll chuckle till stars are shining bright!

The Dance of Dappled Light

The sunbeams waltz on soft green grass,
While dandelions play with sass.
The shadows twirl in a funny plight,
Chasing each other with sheer delight.

"Why is a peach just like a story?"
"Because both can bring you some glory!"
The apricots giggle in a cluster,
Each one blushing, a fruity luster.

A squirrel arrives, and the party ignites,
With acorn caps for hats, they look quite nice.
They twirl and spin, oh what a sight,
As shadows whisper, "This feels just right!"

As moonlight tips its hat and bows,
We salute the night with joyous vows.
In this dance, we've found our flight,
Living like crazy, oh what a night!

Beneath the Blossom's Embrace

In a world where blossoms speak their mind,
Funniest stories you will find.
"Why did the cherry cross the lawn?"
"To get to the puns! Oh, come on!"

A peach prances with flair so bright,
Swaying to tunes that feel just right.
Lemons laugh at silly woes,
While pomegranates strike funny poses.

With petals dancing, we feel alive,
In this humor, our spirits thrive.
"Meet me under the quirky tree,"
The fruit chorus sang in harmony.

Let's toast to laughter, sweet and bold,
These fruity tales never grow old.
In this crazy patch, we find grace,
With joy and laughter, we embrace!

Whispers Beneath the Boughs

The apple told a joke one day,
A pear laughed in a fruity way.
A peach rolled over, snickering bright,
While cherries bounced with pure delight.

A squirrel overheard the fun,
He chirped a pun and then did run.
The branches shook with laughter's cheer,
As critters danced without a fear.

The lemon slipped on grass so green,
And tumbled over, quite the scene!
The laughter echoed high and low,
While tree trunks swayed with joy, aglow.

Together they dream of sunny skies,
Beneath the leaves, where humor flies.
With every rustle, life's a game,
In this wild world, they're all the same.

Echoes of Fruitful Dreams

The bananas tried to start a band,
While grapes just giggled, oh so grand.
A melon strummed a leafy tune,
And berries jigged beneath the moon.

An orange yelled, 'Now that's off-key!'
The apples stared, but let it be.
With every note, they shook in glee,
As shadows danced, wild and free.

The tree trunk whispered tales of yore,
Of every fruit that danced before.
In laughter, dreams began to surge,
As joyous notes began to urge.

The winds would carry tunes so bold,
Of summer tales forever told.
In this fruity space, they gleefully scheme,
Crafting magic from every dream.

Secrets of the Sunlit Grove

In a grove where laughter reigns,
The fig spoke softly of moonlit gains.
While nuts would giggle in their shells,
Sending echoes like joyful bells.

A berry burst with tales of cheer,
'You should've seen that silly deer!'
And all the nuts fell from their posts,
To laugh at what amazed them most.

An elder tree, so wise and stout,
Said, 'Life's a jest, don't leave it out!'
From branch to branch, the gossip flew,
As leaves danced lightly, fresh as dew.

Beneath the boughs, secrets unfold,
In every laugh, a story told.
The grove alive with joy's delight,
Where every day feels just so right.

Beneath the Canopy of Time

A grasshopper who loved to prance,
Taught the daisies how to dance.
With every leap and twist so spry,
The breeze just chuckled, oh my, my!

An owl peeked through the leaves up high,
Watching fruit and flowers amplify.
With each joke shared among the throng,
The trunks would sway and hum along.

The sun would smile from high above,
As branches shared a tale of love.
The laughter echoed through the clime,
Creating magic beneath the time.

In this realm where whimsy swims,
Every heart sings, life brims.
The lesson learned beneath the trees,
Is joy is found in simple pleasantries.

Serafina's Song Amongst the Trees

Serafina sings to the leaves above,
Her voice echoes, full of love.
A squirrel dances, tries to keep beat,
As apples tumble, landing at her feet.

The bees buzz by, in ballet they glide,
While Serafina laughs, with arms open wide.
A rogue raccoon steals a pie from the shelf,
But giggles break out; who can blame himself?

With every note, a bird starts to twirl,
The fun of the orchard makes all heads whirl.
In a crown of blossoms, she strikes a pose,
While sunlight dapples her twinkling toes.

So if you wander to this merry place,
Bring your own tune, join the silly race.
For harmony's found in a joyful spread,
Where laughter takes flight, and worries are shed.

Journeys Through Fragrant Fields

Through fields so fine, they skip and hop,
Chasing butterflies, never want to stop.
A picnic blanket flies up in the air,
While a curious goat sneaks in with flair.

Laughter erupts as they take a seat,
Sandwiches vanish—oh, what a feat!
Is that mustard or a bee on my nose?
A ticklish chase, in playful throes.

With flowers in hair, they waggle and sway,
Twirling 'round daisies to brighten the day.
Suddenly a hiccup, a tumble, a roll,
They end up in clover, both laughing in console.

So dance in the breeze, let the joy unfold,
With friends and a snack, there's magic—behold!
Here every mishap turns laughter in gold,
In fragrant fields rich, funny stories are told.

The Harmony of Harvest

Carts full of pumpkins, what a sight to see,
Bouncing on bumps, giggles fly free.
A scarecrow yawns, with a sleepy grin,
While critters gather, it's time to begin.

Juicy fruits tumble with a soft plop,
As laughter erupts, they can't make it stop.
A watermelon slips, it's a big rolling race,
And everyone's cheering in this lively space.

With cider and donuts, oh what a treat,
Friends trade some jokes while they munch and meet.
A pie starts to wobble, they watch in delight,
As it sails through the air—a real pie-fight!

So when harvest comes, bring your humor and cheer,
For the best kind of bounty is laughter, my dear.
In every sweet bite, there's a story to weave,
Where fun is the harvest, and it's hard to believe.

in the Midst of Stillness

Amidst quiet trees, a toad croaks with glee,
A breeze whispers secrets, just for the free.
Chasing shadows, a cat gives a leap,
As crickets join in, a laugh from the deep.

A fragile leaf sails right by my nose,
Tickling me softly, oh how it glows!
The squirrels debate on the best acorn prize,
While a sly fox gives mischievous eyes.

Beneath the calm sky, daisies start to sway,
As the sun stretches out, bringing warmth to the day.
What's that small rustle? Let's peek and see!
It's just a brave rabbit, shaking with glee.

So pause when you can, let the laughter ensue,
In the quietest moments, find joy that is true.
For under each branch, in the hush of the morn,
Lies a bouquet of smiles, each one newly born.

The Place Where Shadows Play

Beneath the trees, a giggling crowd,
Where squirrels chatter, feeling proud.
A fruit falls near, splat on my shoe,
I laugh, because what else can I do?

A rabbit hops in a silly dance,
While bees buzz around, not a single glance.
I swing on branches, the leaves do sway,
In this circus of nature, I'll gladly stay.

The sun peeks out, a cheeky grin,
While I play hide and seek with my chin.
The apples snicker in vibrant hues,
Inviting me to play, if I choose.

With every step, a chuckle comes forth,
As shadows frolic, revealing their worth.
In this lively spot, where laughter's a must,
I'll be a jester in nature's crust.

A Haven of Ripened Echoes

Among the branches, a joke is spun,
An orange whispers, 'Life's just begun!'
Lemons roll by, saying, 'What's the squeeze?'
While peaches chuckle with a gentle breeze.

Grapes hang low, their gossip is ripe,
'Who wore that hat? It's truly hype!'
I laugh along, with fruit in my hand,
Creating whispers across this wild land.

The nectarines plot a sweet little prank,
While cherries tease with their plump little ranks.
In this haven, where flavors have fun,
Every bite's a giggle, a race to outrun.

As shadows dance, and laughter ignites,
I join the chorus of fruity delights.
With every chuckle, my heart takes flight,
In this patch of joy, everything feels right.

Where Wildflowers Whisper

Wildflowers laugh in colors so bright,
Their giggles float out in the warm, soft light.
Butterflies waltz, a dance on the breeze,
While daisies poke fun at the ticklish bees.

A dandelion sneezes, puffs all around,
Making wishes tumble, then spin to the ground.
Tall sunflowers cheer with their heads held up high,
'You can't touch this!' they tease with a sigh.

Grasshoppers leap, tell jokes in a race,
While a lazy old snail hums a slow pace.
The wildflowers whisper their secrets so sweet,
In this patch of giggles, oh, what a treat!

Beneath the giggling blooms, I lay down my head,
With nature's jokes dancing, I'll never feel dread.
In this giggle garden, where laughter springs free,
Life feels like a joke, oh, what fun it can be!

Embracing the Shaded Path

On a winding trail where laughter runs deep,
I trip on my shoelace, and tumble, not leap.
The trees chuckle softly, as if to say,
'You're not so graceful, but that's okay!'

A hedgehog rolls by, with a comedic flair,
As I wave hi, it puffs up with care.
The stones start to giggle beneath my feet,
As I dance with rhythm, to this funny beat.

In the shade, where shadows weave tales so grand,
With a wink and a wiggle, I extend my hand.
The flowers all whisper, 'Join in our fun,'
As I twirl with delight, kissed by the sun.

Every corner I turn, I meet something new,
A laughing little critter, or a flower in bloom.
In this playful journey, where joy reigns supreme,
I'm wrapped in the laughter, living the dream.

The Orchard's Silent Watch

Beneath each tree, a secret's kept,
The apples giggle while the branches slept.
Bumblebees buzz with a playful thrum,
As squirrels plan heists for a tasty plum.

Old farmer Joe with his crooked grin,
Chasing after mischief, let the games begin!
"Who stole my pears?" he shouts with glee,
While pears drop down, they just laugh with me.

Wind tickles leaves like a feathered friend,
Whispers of laughter, the good times won't end.
Sunlight dances through the boughs so free,
In this lively grove, there's always spree.

Mice throw a party, cheese laid on the ground,
While foxes groove to a jazzy sound.
Under the stars, where silliness reigns,
Nature's own circus, with no restraints!

Nectar of Nostalgia

Sweet memories swirl in the golden light,
Sipping on laughter feels oh-so-right.
Last summer's tales bounce on the breeze,
Whispers of romance between the trees.

A vintage tractor gives a rusty wheeze,
As I dodge low branches, just trying to squeeze.
Old friends gather for apple pie fights,
Splatter and laughter fill all the nights.

Every fruit hiding a childhood prank,
A stash of secrets in a mossy bank.
The hours tumble like marbles down,
In the orchard, joy wears a friendly crown.

Mason jars filled with giggles and dreams,
Reflecting the sun in bright, shiny beams.
Lost in the sweetness of each funny blunder,
Our hearts beat louder than rolling thunder!

The Melodies of Midsummer

Crickets chirping their symphony sweet,
Grasshoppers jump to a lively beat.
Jams and jellies dance in the air,
Pies cooling on windows, no time to spare.

Laughter erupts with each juicy bite,
As cousins declare they can't put up a fight.
"Grab that big one!" the challenge is made,
As they trip and tumble in a fruit-filled parade.

Watermelon seeds flying like darts,
Landing on noses, oh how it starts!
A cheeky raccoon sneaks a late-night snack,
Its eyes full of mischief, a furry little hack.

Fireflies sparkle, a whimsical show,
While the sun dips low, painting all aglow.
This orchard of laughter, stories unfold,
Is a music box filled with joy, pure gold!

Harvesting Daydreams

Baskets overflowing with dreams to share,
Giggling as we gather, without a care.
A pie baking contest turns quite absurd,
With octopus filling? That's the word!

Juggling peaches while dad takes a stance,
"Oh no!" he exclaims, and away they prance!
Splashes of juice paint the faces around,
In this whirlpool of fun, pure joy is found.

Tomatoes wearing tiny hats cause delight,
An ode to silliness, under the moonlight.
With each wholesome laugh, bonds grow so dear,
In this fruity circus, we have no fear.

As dusk settles in, we gather and cheer,
With tales from the trees, growing ever clear.
Every harvest brings treasures we keep,
In the heart of this orchard, it's laughter, not sleep!

Embraced by Nature's Gift

A squirrel stole my sandwich today,
As I gazed at the trees in dismay.
They giggled with each rustling leaf,
While I plotted my snack thief's grief.

Bees buzzed around, quite the jest,
Dancing on blooms, they do their best.
I waved them away with a frantic shout,
But they just laughed, buzzing about.

A crow swooped down, oh what a sight,
He eyed my hat like it was a kite.
I ducked for cover, what a wild chase,
Nature's punchlines leave no trace.

When twilight fell, the moon took stage,
The critters bowed, they set the age.
In this funny realm, such a thrill,
Where all the rules bend to our will.

In Search of Sheltering Beauty

With a picnic basket and crooked grin,
I ventured forth, let the feast begin.
But ants were plotting a coup d'état,
Moving my chips with a flair, saa!

A bird landed near, all eyes on me,
I offered him crumbs for his VIP spree.
He took a peek, then flapped away,
Guess he preferred his own cabaret.

The shadows danced as I sipped my drink,
While the tree leaves whispered, 'What do you think?'
Laughter echoed, mingled with breeze,
Nature seems to love the tease.

As day turned to dusk, the jokes compounded,
With fireflies lighting up, I felt surrounded.
Each flicker a laugh, each twinkle a song,
In this merry gathering, I felt I belong.

A Retreat Where Sameness Meets Contrast

A lawn chair set, my royal throne,
As I surveyed my kingdom, fiercely known.
A cat appeared, with swagger so bold,
Claiming the shade, quite uncontrolled.

The breeze carried whispers, secrets anew,
I chuckled aloud, 'What will they do?'
A lizard popped out to join in the fun,
His tiny antics left me stunned.

The clouds above began their sketch,
Creating shapes, a comedic stretch.
With every giggle from the sun's bright beams,
Nature painted laughter, bursting at the seams.

And just when the sky turned deep blue,
A raccoon came by, looking for stew.
I shared my snacks with a wink and a grin,
In this realm of chaos, we all fit in.

The Breath Beneath the Leaves

Under the arches where laughter blends,
The wilting daisies became my friends.
As I munched on apples, oh what a feast,
A worm peeked out, said, 'At least!'

The sun played hide and seek with the trees,
Tickling the branches with playful breeze.
I tried to dance as shadows shifted,
But tripped on roots, the earth just lifted.

A woodpecker rapped, giving life a score,
While squirrels debated if they'd seen war.
Amid the chaos, I couldn't contain,
Nature's comedy, they never refrain!

As twilight whispered and night set in,
I chuckled softly at the day's spin.
With creatures around, laughter found its way,
In this green realm, forever I'll stay.

The Secret Life of Leaves

Whispers in the breeze, they plot,
A dance of merriment, they've got.
Tickling branches high above,
A leafy chorus, all in love.

Squirrels in tuxedos, they prance,
Conspiring behind the bark with a glance.
Gossiping acorns, they exchange,
Sudden gusts make their plans derange.

Frogs in shades, they croak the score,
While birds critique from the tree top floor.
It's a stage for each nut and sprout,
In this green cabaret, there's no doubt.

They wave their arms when rain is near,
Splashing puddles with total cheer.
On sunny days, they shimmy and sway,
In their leafy world, they laugh all day.

Sunlight Dappled Dreams

Under the blobs of yellow hue,
The ants perform a grandist view.
With tiny hats and marching feet,
They've got a shoeshine that's quite a treat.

The butterflies wear wings of flair,
Twisting and twirling in the air.
They laugh as they chase the lazy bees,
While plotting world domination, if you please.

Beneath this glow, the shadows play,
Caterpillars dream of flying away.
In the warmth of the silly sun's beam,
Every creature giggles, lost in a dream.

This little corner truly gleams,
Full of sweet and zany themes.
Where daisies and dandelions sing,
They share wild tales of blooming spring.

A Canopy of Secrets

Huddled branches, secrets shared,
While cheeky birds mock those who dared.
Each leaf is a witness, each trunk a guard,
Jokes orange and green, they throw quite hard.

The figs and pears hold meetings tight,
To discuss the squirrel's latest flight.
With laughter echoing through sweet air,
Every fruit spills dirt, they don't care!

Underneath this jovial plight,
The shadows chuckle, plotting the night.
Caterpillars wiggle, dreaming grand,
In this green tapestry, they take a stand.

Roots tangled together, they scheme,
For stretchy vines and a prankish dream.
The fauna, flora, in joyful jest,
In this leafy world, they are so blessed.

Echoes from the Blossom

Petals whisper as they fall,
Did you hear the tree's last call?
A ring of laughter, quite absurd,
As flowers gossip, word by word.

Bumblebees hum silly tunes,
Sharing dates with mischievous loons.
Blossoms blush in rainbow hues,
All while planning a grand parade of views.

Thunderous laughter shakes the boughs,
As butterflies take their elegant vows.
To dance through colors, swirls so bright,
Creating joy that fills the twilight.

Each drift of pollen brings a cheer,
In this garden, silly and sincere.
Echoing laughter, nature's song,
In a place where all the fun belongs.

In Twilight's Gentle Fold

As the sun dips low, the crickets play,
Worms dance in circles, they're savvy and gay.
Trees whisper secrets, branches sway,
While raccoons scheme their grand buffet.

A squirrel in shades adjusts his cap,
Planning a heist, it's a cheeky zap.
"Grab the apples!" he gives the cue,
But falls off the branch - just a dumb thing to do!

The moon starts rising, and shadows creep,
A rabbit hops by, napping sheep.
With laughter that echoes, a playful night,
Nature's own jesters delight in the light.

Fireflies waltz in a dazzling dance,
While owls discuss who missed their chance.
A chorus of giggles spills through the trees,
As nature holds court with whimsical ease.

Secrets Sipped with Sweetness

Under lush canopies, bees hum a tune,
Lemonade laughter, beneath the full moon.
Cherries conversing in juicy delight,
While ants are debating their next little bite.

The peaches in gossip, quite juicy and ripe,
Swapping their stories, buzzing with hype.
"Did you see that worm? He thought he could hide,
But the kitten found him, oh, what a ride!"

A picnic is brewing with sandwiches stacked,
But the seagulls swoop down - that's a real act!
"Quick! Cover the cookies!" the children shout loud,
As laughter erupts, a riotous crowd.

In a bubbling pot, marmalade dreams,
Tickling the taste buds with zany extremes.
And all while the fruits sip their sweet little tea,
Life's full of flavors, come join in with glee!

The Song of Sun-Warmed Soil

In fields of laughter, the flowers croon,
Sunflowers wiggle to a bouncy tune.
Carrots are chuckling, sprouting with flair,
While radishes roll, they do not care!

A puddle of mud holds a mud-skipping race,
With beetles in goggles, they speed with grace.
"Oh dear," sighs the cabbage, "what's all this fuss?
Who knew soil had rhythm? It's quite a plus!"

The earthworms giggle, they twist and they twine,
In underground parties, a wiggly line.
"Do we dig deep or break for a snack?
With all this excitement, who's keeping track?"

When the sun dips low and day must end,
The garden's in stitches, no need to pretend.
As the stars take their seats, a raucous choir,
Join the shenanigans, never to tire.

Blossoms Under the Guardian's Gaze

Beneath watchful branches, giggles unfold,
As blossoms conspire in colors so bold.
"Throw a petal!" suggests one with flair,
"Let's tickle some bees in this playful air!"

A mischievous breeze makes the flowers sway,
"Hey, are those bugs here to stay?"
A ladybug winks, "I'm just passing through,
Looking for deals on a shiny dew!"

In the shade, a troll naps, dreaming away,
Who'd rather be fishing than prancing all day.
But watch out! Young sprouts play tricks, oh so sly,
Filling his shoes up with worms on the fly.

Joyful and sweet, the orchard thrives,
As laughter and blossoms wrap up their lives.
In this enchanted Sanctuary, life's a breeze,
With giggles and petals dancing through the trees.

Nourished by Nature's Embrace

Beneath the trees we sit quite snug,
With ants as friends, we give a shrug.
A squirrel steals our juicy treat,
While we laugh at his tiny feet.

The apples drop with a gentle thud,
We dodge the fruits like we're in the mud.
A pie is born from our clumsy hands,
We try to bake, but it rarely stands.

Palette of the Orchard's Bounty

Crimson splashes on the green stage,
Nature's colors, a playful age.
Plum and pear in a fruit buffet,
We're here to munch and laugh all day.

With every bite, a giggle flows,
Juicy drips down to our toes.
A taste of laughter in the air,
We trade our snacks without a care.

The Sweetness that Lingers

Honey drips from the hive with glee,
As bees buzz 'round, they sing to me.
With sticky fingers and silly grins,
We savor sweets while dodging spins.

The sunbeams bounce from leaf to leaf,
In this orchard, we lose our grief.
A sticky hug from a friendly bee,
Clumsy joy fills our hearts with glee.

Beneath the Guardian Branches

Under branches, we play our games,
Pretending to be famous names.
An apple toss, but it hits a dude,
He turns around, we're all quite rude.

The shadows dance with a funny sway,
As we sip our juice and shout hooray.
A secret club in nature's space,
Where laughter blooms, there's no disgrace.

Chronicles of the Orchard

The apples danced in the warm breeze,
A squirrel plotted to steal with ease.
He wore a hat, quite grand and bold,
Chasing tales of treasures untold.

The pears giggled as they swayed,
Creating mischief, oh how they played.
"Let's form a band!" one pear did shout,
The others chimed in, "Let's jam about!"

A ladybug danced on a peach's cheek,
While a worm claimed the fruit was his peak.
"Don't eat me raw!" cried the peach with fright,
"Join our fun, we'll party tonight!"

The trees laughed hard, their branches shook,
Turning pages in a very old book.
Their stories spilled out in sunshine rays,
Crafting laughter in their leafy maze.

Collection of Sunlit Memories

In the sun's glow, the cherries chuckled,
A bumblebee swayed, quite happily buckled.
He claimed to be king of the buzzing crew,
With dreams of a throne made of morning dew.

The strawberries held a juice-tasting show,
Inviting all fruits, "Come on, let's go!"
As pies flew in, with laughter they stuck,
One pie hollered, "I'm out of luck!"

The peaches rolled down, vying for grace,
While plums played tag in their purple space.
"Taste this fruit punch!" one grape did yell,
But all ended up splatted, oh what a smell!

In this garden, silliness thrives,
With giggles and grins among the hives.
Each blossom glittering under the sun,
Making memories of jovial fun.

Beneath the Canopy of Time

Hidden below the trees' embrace,
A rabbit hopped with remarkable grace.
"Hey, look at me!" he proudly proclaimed,
While the hedgehog simply just flamed.

The figs complained of their sticky plight,
"I'm stuck! I'm stuck!" cried one in fright.
Then a bird swooped down with a sing-song tune,
"Join us, let's dance beneath the moon!"

The branches shook with jests and cheer,
Laughter echoed for all to hear.
"Let's play hide and seek," a lemon said,
But no one could find where the walnut fled.

In this playful nook, time seems to flow,
With nature's hilarities putting on a show.
Each leaf whispers tales of bright delight,
In a world where everything feels just right.

Whispered Promises in Petals

Neighbors bloom with riotous glee,
Sharing secrets with a buzzing bee.
"Let's prank the farmer," one daisy grinned,
"Stick a worm in his pocket, let's begin!"

The tulips teamed up for a dance-off,
While sunflowers cheered with a loud scoff.
"Bet you can't sway like we do!"
They challenged the beans, who nodded, "Let's skew!"

A breeze carried whispers of dreams so sweet,
Of lotions brewed from brown beet juice treat.
The fruits chimed in, crafting tales galore,
About haunted trees and their ghostly lore!

In this garden, laughter never wanes,
Tickling toes of all who remains.
Under the sun, where promises are made,
Fun grows freely, in every shade.

Beneath the Fruit-Laden Arms

Beneath the branches, the apples grin,
While pears in pockets try to sneak in.
Cherries gossip, swaying on high,
Claiming the best spots, oh me, oh my!

The cantaloupes tumble, what a delight,
Laughing at lemons who fight for the light.
Berries in clusters exchange cheeky banter,
While oranges plot to become the new dancer.

In the village below, cucumbers jest,
As cabbage heads plot like they're on a quest.
The figs have a meeting; they share a wise tale,
While ripened delights weigh down every rail.

So gather your friends, in laughter we'll bask,
For fruits tell the tales, if only we ask.
With giggles and joy, let's join in this spree,
Under the bounty; it's wild and so free!

Twilight Harmony Among Green

As day melts away, the broccoli plays,
A dance with the radish, in evening's soft rays.
Tomatoes are blushing, feeling quite frisky,
While peas roll their eyes, thinking it's risky.

A pumpkin with flair steals the show near the fence,
While spinach sings low, making whispers intense.
The squash is a jokester, with puns that amuse,
While herbs giggle softly, each with their own views.

At dusk they unite, a melonic parade,
With laughing cucumbers, who aren't ever afraid.
Charming the stars with their leafy delight,
Swaying in rhythm till the fall of the night.

Laughter and chirps fill the cool evening air,
As veggies delight in their funny affair.
In this hilarious garden, they thrive like a team,
Creating a scene straight out of a dream!

Secrets of the Silenced Seedlings

Whispers of seedlings, so shy yet so bright,
Sharing their stories beneath soft moonlight.
They gossip of soil and the worms that they meet,
Trading their secrets while snuggled in sweet.

A carrot once claimed he could jump like a hare,
While beets rolled their eyes, saying, "Don't you dare!"
News of the pumpkin's new hat made a splash,
While beans crack a joke, and the radishes flash.

The chard wears a scarf; it thinks it's so cool,
While peas share their laughs, the funniest fool.
All tucked in the garden where shadows entwine,
Letting their humor and silliness shine.

So listen quite closely to what they might say,
For laughter amongst them can brighten the day.
In the hushed little plot, where the seedlings do dwell,
Funny tales grow strong, in their leafy cartel!

A Meadow's Melodic Shade

In a meadow so green, where giggles abound,
The daisies are planning a dance on the ground.
With butterflies fluttering, they join in the fun,
While bees hum a tune, sweet like fresh-baked bun.

The sunflowers lean in, lending petals to chat,
As clovers wear hats made of leaves and of fat.
A riddle from thistles makes everyone laugh,
While the grass rolls around, executing a gaffe.

The dandelions blow, sending wishes away,
While the daisies tease, "You'll find us one day!"
In this cheery patch, where the wild critters roam,
Nature's own concert, a place called home.

So come along, friends, let's join in and play,
In the laughter and joy, we'll toss cares away.
For in this bright meadow, where silliness reigns,
Life's little quirks bring the sweetest of gains!

Roots of Forgotten Stories

Deep in the soil where secrets creep,
Old moles gossip, make us peep.
A squirrel's dance on branches high,
Tales of fruitcakes that never fly.

Jams and jellies, in jars so bright,
Conspire in shadows, a sweet delight.
When harvest comes and the laughter rolls,
Even the apples play silly roles.

Bug-shaped hats on ants galore,
Plotting heists for fruit they adore.
"Hold the pear!" cries one in a rush,
While the others giggle, plotting their hush.

The whispers of roots, a joke they weave,
Unraveling laughter, who would believe?
Underneath leaves, we all agree,
Orchard life is hilarious, carefree.

A Symphony of Sighs

The breeze hums softly, just for kicks,
While birds critique the latest tricks.
A worm slides by, a slippery chap,
With fruit in mind, he plots a nap.

Caterpillars hold a fashion show,
Strutting their stripes, putting on a glow.
They chuckle and wiggle in perfect sync,
While waiting for butterflies, soft as ink.

Old trees gossip, their branches sway,
"Did you hear that? Another bad day!"
Chirps and chuckles fill the air,
As the sun adds sparkle to their cheeky flair.

Yet in this chaos, harmony reigns,
As laughter echoes through all the lanes.
A symphony made of giggles and sighs,
Where everyone's a star under sunny skies.

Where the Heartwood Grows

In the boughs where dreams take flight,
A fruit fell down with a comical bite.
"That's not a berry," a voice exclaimed,
"More like a disco ball, unashamed!"

Crickets conducting a midnight play,
As fireflies join, lighting the way.
Silly shadows prance on the ground,
With apples rolling, laughter unbound.

A tree branch bows under fruit's weight,
"Can someone help? I'm feeling great!"
The pears chuckle, "We can't assist,
But we can sit back and eat fruit salad bliss."

In this whimsical place where heartwood thrives,
Laughter and joy feel so alive.
Here every fruit has a story to share,
Whirling around without a care.

Cradled by the Canopy

Beneath the leaves, a picnic's begun,
Ants do the cha-cha, oh what fun!
"Pass the lemonade!" a voice calls out,
While everyone giggles, no room for doubt.

A squirrel with style wears a nutty hat,
While pondering if he's chubby or fat.
"Does this apple make me look round?"
The laughter erupts, a joyful sound.

Fragrant pies float in the warm air,
But one brave fruit flies—who knows where?
"I'll catch it!" cries a robin in flight,
Yet collides with a branch, what a sight!

In the whispers above, the fun swells high,
As laughter dances with the fluttering sky.
Cradled by nature's playful embrace,
Every moment we share brings a smile to our face.

www.ingramcontent.com/pod-product-compliance
Lightning Source LLC
Chambersburg PA
CBHW060141230426
43661CB00003B/523